P9-CFX-994

THE MAYA

JACQUELINE DEMBAR GREENE
THE MAYA

Franklin Watts   New York   London   Toronto   Sydney   A First Book

Map by Joe LeMonnier
Cover photograph copyright © Robert Frerck/Odyssey/Chicago
Photographs copyright ©: Peabody Museum, Harvard University, by Hillel Burger: pp. 8, 24,
32, 49; University of Oklahoma Press, (from "The Rise and Fall of the Maya Civilization" by J.
Eric S. Thompson, 1954, 1966): pp. 10, 34; Art Resource, New York: pp. 12, 29, 38 (D. Donne
Bryant), 44 (Giraudon), 46 top, 47 top (both SEF), 47 bottom; Ron Greenberg: pp. 15, 56;
Odyssey Productions/Chicago: pp. 21 (Virginia Miller), 28 (J. J. Foxx), 40, 46 bottom, 54 (all
Robert Frerck); North Wind Picture Archives: p. 26; Dumbarton Oaks, Washington, D.C.:
p. 35; Historical Pictures Service, Chicago: p. 41; Munson-Williams-Proctor Institute, Museum
of Art, Utica, New York: p. 50; Earl Dibble; p. 55.

Library of Congress Cataloging-in-Publication Data

Greene, Jacqueline Dembar.
The Maya / by Jacqueline Dembar Greene.
p. cm.—(A First book)
Includes bibliographical references (p.   ) and index.
Summary: Describes life in this ancient civilization, including
farming techniques, rulers, priests, gods, markets, courts, palaces,
science, letters, and art.
ISBN 0-531-20067-1
1. Mayas—Juvenile literature. [1. Mayas. 2. Indians of Central
America.] I. Title. II. Series.
F1435.G74 1992
972.81′016—DC20   91-29433   CIP   AC

CONTENTS

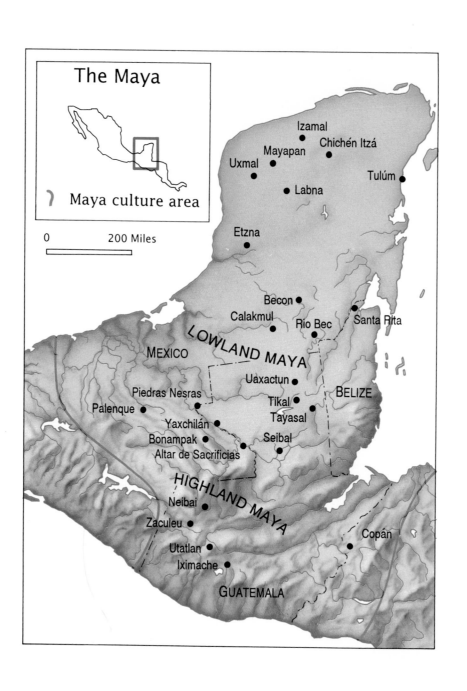

The Maya

Maya culture area

0   200 Miles

Izamal
Chichén Itzá
Mayapan
Uxmal
Tulúm
Labna
Etzna
Becon
Calakmul
Rio Bec
Santa Rita
LOWLAND MAYA
MEXICO
Uaxactun
BELIZE
Piedras Nesras
Tikal
Palenque
Tayasal
Yaxchilán
Bonampak
Seibal
Altar de Sacrificias
HIGHLAND MAYA
Neibai
Zaculeu
Copán
Utatlan
Iximache
GUATEMALA

LIFE IN MAYA LANDS

The first people probably came to Central America as early as 10,000 B.C. They came from Asia, following the great herds of mammoths, mastodons, and buffalo, which were their main source of food. Over many hundreds of years, the climate became drier, grasses withered and died, and the great woolly mammals began to die off.

By 6,000 B.C., the people had to rely more on gathering fruits and plants, and they gradually learned to grow crops for a steady supply of food. As they increased their skills in farming, they also built permanent homes and settled together in villages.

One native group, the Maya, built on the achievements of their ancestors to develop an advanced and thriving civilization. From 300 to 900 A.D. they were at the highest point of their development.

Explorers and scientists have found the remains of Maya cities in areas that are today the countries of Mex-

MAYA PAINTERS DEPICTED LIFE
IN THEIR SEACOAST VILLAGES.

ico, El Salvador, Honduras, Guatemala, and Belize. Some cities were located along seacoasts, and the Maya who lived there became skilled fishermen and canoe travelers. Others lived inland in dense tropical forests, clearing land to grow crops. It is estimated that there were at least two million Maya people at the height of their civilization. Some cities had forty thousand or more living within their boundaries.

Appearance → Maya people had certain physical characteristics in common. They were short and had strong, sturdy builds. The average woman grew to be about 4 feet, 8 inches (1.4 m) tall. The typical man was 5 feet, 1 inch (1.52 m) in height. They all had black hair, dark brown eyes, and dark skin.

In addition to the features the Maya were born with, they developed certain traits that they admired. When a baby was born, its mother bound the infant's head between boards to encourage the soft bones to grow into a long, sloping forehead. This was considered beautiful. When a young man grew up, he often burned the hair off the front of his head to make his slanting forehead more noticeable.

A mother would attach a bright bead to the hair that fell in front of her baby's eyes to create crossed eyes, which was also thought to be attractive. This may have been done to imitate pictures of the sun god, who was always shown with crossed eyes.

Many adults filed their teeth to sharp points. Some wealthy Maya had their front teeth inlaid with round pieces of jade. This was considered becoming and was a sign of high status. Women and men of all classes decorated their bodies with tattoos. The Maya loved jewelry and commonly had their earlobes, lips, and one nostril pierced so that they could wear large ornaments.

The Maya did not need heavy clothing in the hot,

TALENTED ARTISTS ALWAYS DREW MAYA
FACES IN PROFILE. PERHAPS THEY
WANTED TO EMPHASIZE FEATURES THAT
WERE CONSIDERED THE IDEAL
OF BEAUTY, SUCH AS A SLOPING
FOREHEAD AND A PROMINENT NOSE.

humid climate. They grew cotton plants, and women were skilled at spinning cotton into thread and weaving it into cloth. Sometimes they painted fabric with vegetable dyes or embroidered decorative designs.

Men wore loincloths with long panels hanging in front and back. Wealthy men had their loincloths intricately embroidered. Women wore skirts tightly wrapped around their waists, paired with long loose blouses. They might also wear loose dresses, like smocks. Frequently, they embroidered the dresses around the necks and hems with designs of flowers or birds. On cool days or evenings, men and women wrapped blankets around their shoulders.

The clothing of the upper classes was remarkable for its decorative quality. Men wore delicate, elaborate headdresses, usually with long, colorful feathers. They also wore breastplates and many rings, earplugs, nose ornaments, and necklaces. The average Maya walked barefoot or wore simple sandals woven of straw. The wealthy wore ornate sandals made of leather or thick fiber.

Raising Children → In Maya families, children were a sign of good fortune. When a baby was born, a priest was called in to give the child a sacred name and to predict its future. Newborn infants were carried in their mothers' arms. As the baby grew bigger, the mother

THIS SCENE SHOWS MAYA
NOBLEMEN WEARING ELABORATE FEATHER
HEADDRESSES AND LOINCLOTHS.

shifted it to rest against her left hip. Soon the child was given a family nickname and a formal last name that combined the parents' names.

When a girl turned five, her mother tied a string around her waist with a red shell attached. This ornament stayed until she was initiated into adolescence at age twelve. When boys turned five, a white bead was braided into their hair. It remained until their initiation ceremony at age fourteen. A priest chose the most favorable day for an initiation ceremony. Afterward, the priest cut the bead from a boy's hair. A girl's mother cut the string from her daughter's waist. Then parents hosted a family celebration. They gave gifts, and guests would eat and drink.

A girl's life didn't change much after her initiation ceremony. She continued to live with her parents and learned to cook, preserve foods, spin cotton yarn, weave, and clean house.

An unmarried girl learned to behave according to Maya customs. She lowered her eyes and stepped aside when she passed a man on the street. She was taught that a woman served her husband his meals and ate only after he had finished. A girl's parents arranged her marriage two or three years after her initiation ceremony.

After his initiation, a boy moved from his family's home to a communal house shared by several young men. He spent most of his days working in the fields with his father and learning crafts, games, and warfare. When he was about eighteen, a young man's parents arranged for his marriage. They offered gifts of cotton cloth, tobacco, and cocoa beans to the bride's family.

Just before a marriage, a couple's friends and relatives helped build them a new hut. Then they filled it with household presents, such as wooden chests and woven bags for storage, cooking pots, water gourds, baskets, and a *metate*, or grinding stone, for corn.

A Maya priest performed the marriage ceremony, and the bride's father provided a wedding banquet. While common people usually took one marriage partner for life, a wealthy man often had several wives. This meant he would have many people to keep his house in order and prepare his meals. It also ensured that he would be blessed with many children.

Palaces and Huts → Maya cities served as centers for markets, courts, and religious ceremonies. Some cities were connected to each other by wide paved roads that were used for religious processions and by traders from other regions. The Maya also built some *aqueducts* and drainage systems to carry waste water away.

At the center of each city were huge stone pyramids topped with temples. Priests used the temples for important festivals and religious ceremonies. Near the bases of the pyramids, stone palaces with many rooms were built. These were probably used by the priests as their sleeping quarters and as places to study.

The most desirable place to live was close to the center of the city. A person's status was reflected in the location of his house. Wealthy Maya lived in *stucco*-covered stone houses near the temples. Their homes were large and had many cool, comfortable rooms divided by cotton drapes. Rooms were frequently built around a

HOW MAYA RUINS LOOK TO US TODAY

private central patio. Some houses were decorated on the outside with large plaster figures of gods to show that the house was under divine protection.

Well-to-do families enjoyed many comforts. Their beds were built on raised platforms and covered with soft cushions and cotton sheets. Clothing and household items were neatly stored in wooden chests, on shelves, or in net bags that hung from pegs. Servants prepared meals and kept the house clean and in good repair.

Farther from the city center, merchants and craftsmen had modest but comfortable homes. They were skilled in pottery making, basket weaving, or stonework and were considered part of a respected professional middle class.

Farmers lived farthest from the cities in huts close to their fields. A hut could be oval, square, or rectangular in shape. Walls were made of thin wooden poles tied together tightly with vines. Sometimes a layer of mud covered the walls, but most often they were left with natural spaces that allowed air to circulate. The thatched roofs were made of palm leaves or long grasses, and a small hole allowed smoke from cooking fires to escape.

Usually farmers' huts had only one room and an earth floor. One end of the room held low wooden beds covered with straw mats. The cooking hearth was at the opposite end. Sometimes the room was divided by poles or a cotton sheet to separate the two sections.

Often several huts were built around one central courtyard. Usually these were family compounds, but they could be shared by unrelated families. This arrangement made it easier to share daily tasks, and men frequently worked together in the fields for the benefit of all.

Most families kept animals for pleasure and for food. Spider monkeys were favorite pets, as were *coatis*, which are raccoon-like animals. Turkey, ducks, and deer were kept for food at special feasts. Turkey feathers were often used for decoration or to weave into sleeping mats for extra warmth on cold nights. The Maya raised several types of dogs, including a unique variety that did not bark. Dogs were probably not pets but were used as ceremonial food and for sacrifices at special religious rituals.

The Maya kept their homes clean and free of trash. Each family collected its trash and took it to a community dump. This material was recycled by using it as filler when a new building was constructed.

Farming → The Maya developed sophisticated farming techniques. In many areas, farmers terraced hillsides, creating flat steps to hold rows of plants. In low areas, where fields might be flooded, they built up the soil to create drier, raised fields. In dry areas, the Maya dammed waterways to create reservoirs and dug irrigation ditches to keep fields watered.

Farmers used stone axes to remove trees and clear land for planting. They used the *slash-and-burn* method to clear the remaining underbrush. They created fire by causing friction with a wooden drill and burned the thick brush. Because the soil was poor, the Maya left the remaining ash for fertilizer. They made holes in the top layer of ash with wooden poles and dropped in seeds. After a year or two, the soil was depleted and the field had to be abandoned until the fertility had returned.

The Maya believed the souls of corn plants would move to cleaner fields if weeds were allowed to grow. Therefore, abandoned fields were left to return to jungle growth. The farmer moved to another area and cleared new land.

The farmer's main crop was corn, or *maize*. He weeded plants daily to keep the gods happy and to ensure a good harvest. Beans were planted in the same hole as corn seeds. As the bean vine grew, it wrapped itself around the corn plant, which gave it support. The farmer also planted *henequen,* a plant used to make rope, and cotton, tobacco, sweet potatoes, cocoa beans, squash, gourds, chili peppers, tomatoes, pumpkins, and *jícima,* a type of turnip eaten raw.

The Maya also cultivated orchards of avocado trees,

whose fruit provided a good source of protein. Papayas, bananas, nuts, and plantain grew wild. The people kept hives of stingless bees in hollow logs for a steady supply of honey. Many modern Maya still keep bees with the same methods used by their ancestors.

The people's diet was mainly vegetarian, as meat was eaten only on special occasions. Yet their food supplied enough vitamins and protein. In later times, they ground corn on metates and made thin cakes that were fried on a flat stone. These *tortillas* are still the main part of a modern Maya diet.

In good times, farmers produced more than they needed to feed their families. Whether harvests were good or bad, a portion was given to priests and members of the upper class, who were never expected to work in the fields. They felt the land belonged to them, and the farmers gave them a portion of the harvest for the privilege of using it.

Trade was an important activity of Maya culture, and food was among the items actively traded with people from other areas. Maya living in the jungle areas offered the edible hearts of palm trees. People closer to the ocean, particularly in the Yucatan Peninsula of Mexico, traded salt and dried fish. Some things were bartered, others bought for cocoa beans, used as money. Rich people showed off their wealth by grinding the beans into powder and drinking it as cocoa.

RULERS, PRIESTS, AND GODS

Archaeologists have much more to learn about Maya government, but some information has been established. Each large city had one supreme chief who usually ruled over the city and the surrounding region for life. Upon his death, a son or brother took over. In some cases, the ruler's wife might be next in line. If no family successor was available, a new ruler was chosen from the upper class.

Each Maya city-state also had several less important chieftains, who served in jobs somewhat like our mayors. These men might have had other full-time occupations as well.

Chieftains also served as judges, and there were prescribed punishments for certain crimes. A thief became the servant of his victim. Murderers were put to death, sometimes as part of a ritual sacrifice. For minor crimes, a criminal's hair was cut off as a sign of disgrace.

THIS FLAT STONE SLAB CALLED
A STELA SHOWS A RULER HOLDING
A SYMBOL OF HIS OFFICE.

There was a definite separation between the life of the ruling class and that of the common people. Certain luxury items, such as jade, feathers, and jaguar pelts, were only to be used by members of the ruling class. It was the job of the commoners to provide these items as offerings. When members of the upper class traveled, workers were expected to carry them in *litters*.

Warriors were a separate class, whose main goal was to capture enemy prisoners. Sometimes farmers and other members of the lower class were forced to serve as soldiers. Captured enemy soldiers became slaves. Defeated officers became human sacrifices.

Armies did not begin fighting until after an elaborate religious ceremony. Warriors wore feathered headdresses, and many carried bright pennants. In battle, soldiers carried shields made from thick animal hides. They fought with wooden clubs, flint knives, spears, and slingshots. Warriors were also known to use hornet bombs, in which a hornet's nest was thrown into a group of enemy soldiers.

All fighting stopped each evening, and there was a truce until morning. If an army's commander was seriously wounded or killed, his army retreated and the battle ended.

What They Believed → Religion was a strong force in Maya life and regulated almost everything. Because of its importance, priests were the highest class of citizens. Frequently, they were also ruling chiefs. Only priests were educated to know all of the gods, prayers, and rituals. Ordinary people were not allowed to enter the temples. They participated only in religious festivals honoring their everyday gods, under the direction of priests.

The Maya believed the gods had destroyed and re-created the earth several times, and they believed this cycle would happen again. Perhaps that is why they tried to please the gods. It may also be why they became fearful when natural events, such as droughts, made them think the gods were angry.

All Maya gods were related to nature. Sunrise and sunset, rainfall and sunshine—all were important to the people's survival, so it isn't surprising that they believed gods controlled all of the elements.

The Supreme Being and creator of the universe was a kind god named *Hunab Ku*. The next most important gods were those of the sun and moon. The Maya thought all people were descended from them. The sun god was the "father" of the Maya people. He was depicted with crossed eyes. The moon god was the wife of the sun and the Maya "mother." She watched over women's lives. She helped them with their weaving and household duties and brought them good fortune when their children were born.

The corn god was responsible for a successful har-

THIS SCULPTURE OF THE HEAD
OF THE MAIZE GOD WEARS A HEADDRESS
DEPICTING EARS OF CORN.

vest. Statues show him wearing a headdress made of ears of corn. The god of death was fearsome and powerful. He was shown with a skeleton face and spine.

Four rain gods, called *Chacs,* controlled rainfall, thunder, lightning, and storms. Like the corn god, the Chacs were especially important to farmers. There were special gods for trade, hunting, war, poetry, and sacrifices. Every job or activity in Maya life had a patron god.

Sacrifices to the Gods → A common practice in Maya religion was to offer a sacrifice to please the gods. At nearly every ceremony and festival, incense made from a yellow resin called *copal* was burned, and its fragrance filled the air. The people believed that blood was required in a ritual sacrifice. Priests sometimes drew their own blood for special ceremonies, but animals, particularly dogs and birds, were most often victims.

Human sacrifice was performed when priests felt there was a great need to appease the gods, such as during a long drought. They believed sacrifice of a person was the greatest offering. People used in these bloody rituals were primarily captured prisoners, slaves, and criminals. Some victims may have been volunteers. Children were sometimes sacrificed as they were considered pure and innocent. These children were mostly orphans,

A KNEELING WOMAN PERFORMS A BLOOD
SACRIFICE BEFORE THE RULER SHIELD JAGUAR
AT THE TEMPLE IN YAXCHILÁN.

but some were kidnapped or bought from families in other cities.

An important ritual involving human sacrifice, was performed at the site of a *cenote,* a deep limestone well. The cenotes were believed to be the homes of gods who could predict the amount of rainfall for the coming year.

For sixty days before a cenote sacrifice, priests and their victims prayed and purified themselves. As dawn broke on the morning of the sacrifice, priests threw the victims into the well. They also dropped in offerings of valuable items. Most of the victims drowned, but if there were any survivors by noontime, they were pulled out and asked what messages the gods had sent them about rainfall.

In the early 1900s, the American explorer Edward Herbert Thompson wanted to find out more about the Well of Sacrifice in the Maya city of Chichén Itzá in Mexico. Wearing heavy diving gear, he had himself lowered into the depths of the cenote. At the bottom, he gathered up human skulls and bones, pieces of clothing, spear throwers and stone knives, pottery, small copper bells, jade, gold bowls, beads, and carved figures.

The Importance of Priests → Religion gave meaning and order to the lives of the Maya. It answered their questions about the mysteries of nature and gave them the feeling that they had some control over their lives.

AN AERIAL VIEW OF A CENOTE,
WHERE HUMAN SACRIFICES WERE
PERFORMED. A TEMPLE LOOMS
IN THE DISTANCE.

RELIGION PLAYED A SIGNIFICANT
ROLE IN MAYA SOCIETY, AND PRIESTS,
SUCH AS THE ONE PICTURED ABOVE,
WERE ITS MOST IMPORTANT CITIZENS.

Priests became extremely powerful because they connected people to the gods. Priests also understood the complicated writing and calendar systems, explained important events, and predicted the future.

New priests were chosen from the sons of older priests and upper-class families. These young men spent a long time studying and training, and they entered priesthood for life. Girls could enter religious orders to care for the temples and keep the sacred fires burning, but they could not become priests. They could leave their order at any time.

There were several types of priests, classified according to their duties. The highest group trained younger priests in ritual, science, and prophecy. Others studied calendars and predicted the future. Two orders of priests assisted in sacrifices. Finally, there were priests who knew special prayers and cures for sick people. The Maya thought illness was caused by evil spirits and the gods' disfavor. They believed some people went to paradise after they died, including women who died in childbirth, warriors killed in battle, victims of sacrifice, priests, and those who had lived good lives.

Priests organized many exciting religious festivals for the people. Clowns and storytellers entertained, musicians played, and masked actors performed plays. Copal incense was offered, and there were prayers, chants, and ritual dancing. Priests sacrificed food and animals on the temple steps. People feasted and drank a fermented corn beverage that occasionally led to drunkenness.

SCIENCE, LETTERS, AND ART

One of the most important jobs of priests was to study the seasons of the year and calculate time. To do this, they became highly skilled in the use of numbers. They also studied stars and planets and were excellent astronomers.

The city of Copán, in Honduras, was a center of Maya astronomy and had a high structure used as an observatory. Although their only known tool for studying the heavens was a pair of crossed sticks, the priests were able to record the precise movements of the sun, the moon, and the planet Venus.

The astronomer-priests at Copán established a lunar calendar (based on the cycles of the moon) and a solar calendar (based on the sun). As an example of Maya skills, scientists today point out that the Maya solar year was almost exactly the same as our 365-day-year. In addition, the Maya were able to determine the orbit of

THIS RECONSTRUCTION SHOWS WHAT THE CITY
OF COPÁN IN HONDURAS LOOKED LIKE, WITH ITS
BROAD PLAZA AND TALL PYRAMID TEMPLES.

Venus and other planets. They were able to predict accurately eclipses of the sun and the moon, to the people's amazement.

The Maya Calendars → Because of their advanced system of astronomy and use of numbers, the Maya were able to create a complicated calendar system to record past, present, and future events. It is believed that the basic unit of these calendars was the day and that they did not keep time in hours, minutes, or seconds.

Priests established three basic calendars. There was a civil calendar of 365 days for everyday affairs and the times of planting and harvest. There was a sacred calendar, called the _tzolkin,_ (meaning "the count of days") for religious and ceremonial events. It had a cycle of 260 days. There was a third calendar that was made up of 360 days. This calendar was used primarily for the _Long Count,_ a special Maya system used to keep track of longer time spans, similar to the way we measure decades and centuries.

The Maya people depended on priests to predict whether each day was lucky or unlucky and to make long-range forecasts about whether the gods would give favor to their lives. To assist in their forecasts, priests developed a system called the _Calendar Round._ It connected the 365-day civil calendar with the 260-day sacred

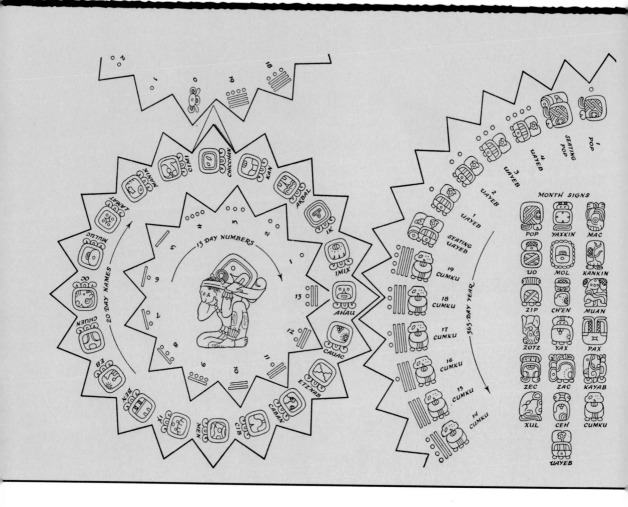

THE MAYA HAD AN INTRICATE
SYSTEM FOR RECORDING TIME.
TO CALCULATE DATES,
THE PRIESTS USED A
SOPHISTICATED KNOWLEDGE
OF MATHEMATICS.

A MAYA BOWL DEPICTING THE SHELL GOD.
THIS WAS THE MAYA DEITY WHO RULED
OVER THE FIVE UNLUCKY INTER-
CALENDARY DAYS AT THE END OF THE YEAR.
PART OF THE GLYPH OVER HIS HEAD
APPARENTLY REPRESENTS A SHELL, AND
THE WHOLE GLYPH MIGHT HAVE RECORDED
HIS NAME. HE IS USUALLY
REPRESENTED AS AN OLD MAN.

calendar, giving thousands of different combinations. This calendar was considered important for many rituals.

The Number System → The calendar system and the study of the stars and planets could not have been accomplished without a sophisticated understanding of mathematics. Children of the upper classes studied the use of numbers as part of their education, and priests were constantly using numbers to make their calculations and predictions.

The Maya used a system of dots and lines to write numbers. Each dot represented 1. A horizontal bar line represented 5. A number was read by adding the dots and lines together. For example, three dots indicated the number 3. A line with three dots on it would represent the number 8. Three horizontal lines would equal 15.

Perhaps the most important symbol the Maya used in their mathematics represented zero. A symbol meaning "nothing" is a highly advanced mathematical concept. Although scientists are not absolutely certain that the Maya invented the zero, they were the first people in the Americas to use it. This symbol was not used in Europe until hundreds of years later.

Mayas recorded the numeral o in three principal ways. They often used a *glyph,* or picture symbol, of a shell. At others times they used a hand glyph. Sometimes they represented zero with the symbol of a head.

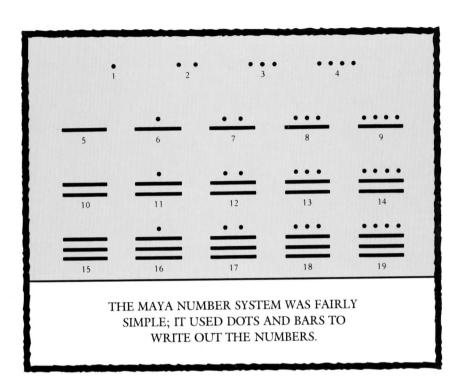

THE MAYA NUMBER SYSTEM WAS FAIRLY
SIMPLE; IT USED DOTS AND BARS TO
WRITE OUT THE NUMBERS.

The use of zero allowed the Maya to calculate extremely large numbers. Some of the numbers they recorded in the Long Count add up to as much as 400,000,000.

Written Language → Scientists think the Maya had the most advanced writing system of all native American groups. Mayas recorded their language by using a system of *hieroglyphics,* which are picture symbols. These symbols represented either sounds, ideas, or individual

HIEROGLYPHICS WERE CARVED
ON STONE OR PAINTED ON BARK
TO RECORD MAYA HISTORY,
CUSTOMS, AND LITERATURE.

words. There were so many different symbols that only priests and rulers knew them all.

Glyphs usually were written in horizontal rows and read from left to right. Sometimes they were written in vertical columns and read from top to bottom.

The Maya recorded information on flat stone slabs called *stelae*. Carved stone columns decorated the doorways of temples and monuments and recorded historical events and important dates. Carvings are also found on altars and stairs. Glyphs were cut into the stone by skilled craftsmen, who had only simple stone tools for their work. Yet the glyphs are filled with delicate detail, and there is rarely a mistake.

Scribes also painted glyphs on walls and pottery. In addition, they created elaborate written books called *codices* (singular form, *codex*). The books were made of paper from strips of fig-tree bark. To strengthen it, the bark was coated with gum resin, then painted with a thin layer of smooth, white stucco. Skilled scribes drew figures and symbols with colored paint made from various vegetables and minerals. When the writing was completed, the strips were folded like a fan and enclosed between two wooden or leather covers.

The Maya probably had an extensive collection of books about their customs, rituals, science, and literature, but only three have survived. They have been useful in helping archaeologists decipher some of the eight

STONECUTTERS RECORDED EVENTS ON HUGE
STONE PANELS CALLED STELAE. THIS
ONE IS FROM THE EIGHTH CENTURY A.D.

A PAGE FROM THE DRESDEN CODEX,
THE BEST EXISTING EXAMPLE OF
THE MAYA CODICES. THE PAGE
SHOWS A SECTION OF A "TONALAMATL,"
A SACRED RECORD OF DAYS, USED TO
MAKE PREDICTIONS ABOUT THE FUTURE.

hundred different glyphs that have been discovered, but scholars think the lost books contained the key to understanding Maya culture. Unfortunately, when the Spanish invaded Maya lands, a priest named Friar Diego de Landa believed the books were the source of evil beliefs. In 1562, he ordered the books burned.

Art and Music → The artistic creations of the Maya were closely related to religion. Every detail of each god was carefully depicted. Some carvings show religious ceremonies.

Brightly colored paintings decorated stucco walls. Some paintings showed battle scenes and others represented ceremonies involving rulers or priests, but there are few illustrating the life of the common people.

The Maya were familiar with the natural life around them, and elements of the environment are shown in their art. Plants were so accurately drawn, as were animals such as birds and snakes, that today scientists can identify many of them.

Artists usually depicted gods, priests, rulers, and mythical figures with the head in profile. This style may have been adopted so that the artist could accentuate the sloping forehead and hooked nose the Maya favored.

Besides sculptors and painters, the Maya had other skilled artisans. Potters made bowls, plates, jugs, and vases that were decorative as well as sturdy. Some pottery was quite large and was probably used to store food or water. Many pieces stood on legs, and most had well-fitting lids. Weavers made cotton cloth, and basket makers and leather workers also created much-needed items. Stones, bones, and shells were polished and made into ornaments. Mosaic pieces—cut stones or tiles set together to form an inlaid design—also were fashioned.

Music was an important part of Maya life, particularly during ceremonies and religious festivals. There was singing, and several types of instruments have been found. For rhythm, there were drums, gourd rattles, and tortoise shells beaten with deer antlers. Trumpets made from conch shells, wooden and reed flutes, and various seashells added to the melodies. In some parts of Mexico and Central America, the ancient music of the Maya is still played and sung.

Architecture → Perhaps the most striking feature of Maya cities is the high stone pyramids built to honor gods and chiefs. At the top of each pyramid is a temple, usually having two or three small rooms. To add to the impressive image of the temple rising toward the sky, Maya architects sometimes added an openwork stone crest at the very top.

Most pyramids were about 70 feet (21 m) tall, with steep, narrow stairs leading up the sides. Sometimes

THE MAYA WERE FINE ARTISANS.
THIS VASE IS A GOOD EXAMPLE
OF MAYA POTTERY.

pyramids had secret burial chambers and hidden passageways in the lower level, where archaeologists have found the remains of important rulers or priests. Often burial chambers are filled with rich offerings to the gods, such as jewelry, gold bowls, and jade statues. Sometimes the bodies of close relatives or servants are found buried with the dead leader.

Pyramids were built on ground level, starting with a large base. They were built up in narrower and narrower layers and then finished with a row of flat stones. A small temple was built at the top. Its rooms were small, dark, and damp because there were no windows; narrow doorways provided the only source of light and air.

Besides working in the fields to produce food for the community, peasants were expected to volunteer their labor to build the pyramids. Construction was a major undertaking, requiring months or even years of effort. Thousands worked together to clear the land, level the ground, and cut the stones that would be used for building.

It is hard for us to imagine how such huge structures could have been built without modern machinery. The Maya did everything by hand. They had no domesticated animals, such as horses or oxen, and they had no wagons or wheels for moving heavy loads. Large blocks

MAYA ARCHITECTURE WAS QUITE DISTINCTIVE AND ESPECIALLY KNOWN FOR ITS PYRAMIDS AND TEMPLES.

A) TEMPLE IN THE YUCATAN
B) THE TEMPLE OF THE WARRIORS AT CHICHÉN ITZÁ, WITH A STATUE OF THE ANCIENT GOD-KING QUETZALCOÁTL, THE FEATHERED SERPENT
C) AN ASTRONOMICAL OBSERVATORY IN CHICHÉN ITZÁ
D) THE TEMPLE OF THE WARRIORS

of limestone were cut and then moved to the building site on rolling logs or carried in slings made of rope.

Pyramids were constructed one level at a time. Rough stones were laid into place, and laborers cemented them together, filling cracks with rubble and trash. This level was smoothed over with plaster before the next tier was begun. Skilled masons fitted the outside of pyramid walls with cut blocks of limestone. This outside wall was then covered with smooth limestone plaster or stucco.

When construction was completed, sculptors using stone tools and wooden mallets carved huge stelae to record the date and the important event or ruler that the pyramid honored. These stone tablets were usually placed at the entrance to the temple. Temple walls were often left with blank white stucco, but frequently artists painted them with images of gods or murals showing battle scenes or important events.

The Ball Court → The best known Maya game is a ball game that was played by skilled men. In almost every Maya city studied by archaeologists, there is at least one ball court, usually located near the temples in the center of the city. The rules of the game varied at different times and in different locations. The court was bordered on two sides by smooth walls. Some versions featured a

THIS PAINTING SHOWS A BALL COURT,
FOUND IN ALMOST EVERY MAYA CITY.
A GAME CALLED POK-A-TOK WAS PLAYED BY
SKILLED MEN AND ENJOYED BY SPECTATORS.

THIS SCULPTURE SHOWS A NOBLEMAN
WEARING BALL-PLAYING CLOTHES,
INCLUDING A PROTECTIVE GARMENT
MADE FROM A JAGUAR HIDE.

high stone ring, hanging vertically, through which the players tried to pass a solid rubber ball.

The game, which may have been called *pok-a-tok*, was played by two teams. Each player wore thick, heavy padding for protection and was allowed to use only his knees, hips, shoulders, or forearms to hit the ball. The ball was not allowed to touch the ground. Scientists guess that the game was so difficult that scoring was rare. Perhaps the first team to score was declared winner.

The Maya believed that the game was a favorite sport of the gods, and some matches were treated as religious ceremonies. There were many rituals to be performed to prepare for a game. It is also possible that losing players sometimes became human sacrifices. Decorations on a ball court at the Maya site of Chichén Itzá in Mexico show players being beheaded.

The games were a popular pastime for the people, and many came out to watch. Spectators placed bets on the outcome, and some risked losing precious possessions, like jewelry, homes, and even children. When the game ended, viewers immediately ran from the court area. According to custom, winning team members could take whatever jewelry, clothing, or other valuable items the spectators had with them.

THE END OF MAYA CITIES

Sometime around 900 A.D., the great Maya cities were abandoned one by one. Although archaeologists are not certain why, there are many possible explanations. Some believe the common people revolted because rulers' demands for food and labor became too great. There may have been a famine that caused widespread sickness and death. There is also some evidence that warrior tribes may have attacked the cities and villages, perhaps in a search for a new supply of food.

Slowly, the decline continued, and by 1450 all major cities were abandoned. Religion became less important. There was less time for art and architecture and more time spent at war. People who survived probably lived in small groups in the countryside.

Invasion by Spain → After the great period of Maya civilization, Spanish explorers invaded in search of new

[52]

lands and gold. The first encounter between the two peoples came in 1502 and was a peaceful one. Christopher Columbus came upon a group of traders off the coast of Honduras, and his son wrote about the chance meeting in his journal. Before long, however, the Spanish attacked the Maya with horses and guns. It was the first time the Maya had seen white people, men on horseback, or modern weapons. They could not fight back successfully.

Arrival of the Spanish marked the final decline of Maya civilization. The native people were exposed to new diseases, such as measles and smallpox, to which they had no natural resistance. Thousands died. Those who survived were sold into slavery or reduced to poverty.

By 1549, representatives of the Spanish Inquisition set up Catholic churches in Mexico and Central America to convert the remaining Maya. A Franciscan friar, Diego de Landa, observed their religious practices and was shocked by human sacrifices. De Landa tried to force the Maya to convert to Christianity. He destroyed temples, had Maya books burned, and tortured and killed many people.

Present-Day Maya → Those who survived the Spanish attacks moved deep into the safety of the jungle. Today there are more than two million Maya, one of the larg-

A COLORFUL MARKET IN GUATEMALA.
LIKE THEIR ANCESTORS, MANY
PRESENT-DAY MAYA ARE
SKILLED CRAFTSPEOPLE.

MANY ANCIENT MAYA SITES HAVE BEEN
RESTORED, AND PEOPLE FROM ALL
OVER THE WORLD COME TO SEE
THE REMNANTS OF THIS REMARKABLE
CIVILIZATION. THIS WAS THE CENTER
OF THE CITY OF TIKAL,
A TRULY MAGNIFICENT SITE.

A PYRAMID TEMPLE AT CHICHÉN ITZÁ
WITH A SCULPTURE OF CHAC,
ONE OF THE MAYA RAIN GODS

est surviving native American cultures. Yet much of their history has been lost, and they live in poverty in the same areas where they once thrived.

Their daily life mirrors that of their ancestors. They live in cool thatched huts that are simply furnished with sleeping hammocks, a low table and benches, a corn-grinding mill, and a stone slab for cooking tortillas. Women still eat separately, after the men have had their fill.

A variety of Maya dialects are still spoken, and some religious customs have been handed down through the centuries. Although most individuals also practice Christianity, Maya religion still plays a large role in their lives. They have kept their passion for ball games, but now the favorite sport is baseball.

Beginning in 1785, scientists and archaeologists began to uncover ruins of great Maya cities in an effort to learn more about the history and culture that once thrived there. Today many sites have been restored and made into national monuments, and the work continues. Visitors to Chichén Itzá, Palenque, and Tulúm in Mexico and to the magnificent sites of Tikal in Guatemala and Copán in Honduras can climb the narrow pyramid steps and walk in the footprints of an ancient people.

GLOSSARY

Aqueduct—a system for allowing water to flow from one location to another

Archaeologist—a scientist who learns about past cultures by studying the items left behind, such as housing, pottery, tools

Calendar Round—a calendar system that combined the 365-day civil calendar with the 260-day sacred calendar; it was used for planning important rituals; the combined day names were used for giving newborn babies their formal, religious names

Cenote (seh-note´-ee)—a deep, natural limestone well

Chacs—four rain gods who controlled rain, thunder, lightning, and storms

Coati (ko-ah´-tee)—a small, raccoon-like animal with a long snout

Codices (singular, codex)—books written by the Maya about their customs, rituals, science, and literature

Copal—a resin from some tropical trees that the Maya burned as fragrant incense

Glyph—a picture symbol of a sound or an object

Henequen (hen'-uh-kin)—a fiber made from the leaves of a tropical plant; used for making strong rope

Hieroglyphics—a system of picture symbols

Hunab Ku—a kind god, thought by Maya to be the Supreme Being and creator of the universe

Jicima (hih'-cum-uh)—root from a Mexican vine, similar to a turnip; it can be eaten raw or cooked.

Litter—a chair with long horizontal bars along the bottom for carrying an honored person

Long Count—a calendar system used for keeping track of long periods of time

Maize—corn

Metate (meh-tah'-tay)—a stone used for grinding corn into flour

Pok-a-tok—a Maya ball game, similar to basketball

Slash-and-burn—a method of clearing jungle for planting crops in which the area is burned and the ashes used to fertilize the soil

Stelae—large stone slabs that were carved with hieroglyphics and used to decorate temple doorways; stelae usually recorded the special date and event to which the temple was dedicated.

Stucco—plaster used to coat building walls

Tortillas—flat cakes made of ground corn and water and fried on a hot stone

Tzolkin (zole'-kin)—the "count of days," a sacred calendar used for religious ceremonies

FOR FURTHER READING

Benson, Elizabeth P. *The Maya World*. New York: Thomas Y. Crowell, 1977.

Henderson, John S. *The World of the Ancient Maya*. Ithaca, N.Y.: Cornell University Press, 1981.

McKissack, Patricia. *Mayas*. Chicago: Children's Press, 1987.

Meyer, Carolyn, and Charles Gallencamp. *The Mystery of the Ancient Maya*. New York: Margaret McElderry Books, 1985.

Odijk, Pamela. *Mayas*. New York: Silver Burdett Press, 1990.

Pine, Tillie S., and Joseph Levine. *The Maya Knew*. New York: McGraw-Hill Book Co., 1971.

Van Hagen, Victor W. *Maya, Land of the Turkey and Deer*. Cleveland, Ohio: World Press, 1960.

INDEX

ABOUT THE AUTHOR

Jacqueline Dembar Greene worked as a reporter and feature writer for several years before she turned to writing for young people. She is the author of eight books. Her picture book, *Butchers and Bakers, Rabbis and Kings,* was a finalist for the National Jewish Book Award. The historical novel, *Out of Many Waters,* was named a Sydney Taylor Honor Book. At present she is working on a sequel to that novel, set in Amsterdam in 1654. Her most recent picture book is *What His Father Did.*

Raised in the small town of Bloomfield, Connecticut, Mrs. Greene earned a B.A. in French literature from the University of Connecticut, and an M.A. in English literature from Central Missouri University. She is married and the mother of two sons and makes her home in Wellesley, Massachusetts. An avid traveler, Mrs. Greene has visited numerous Native American sites in the south-western United States and Mexico. Her books on the Maya and on the Chippewa of the Great Lakes region reflect her desire to share her respect for these native cultures.